Nestlé Smarties ®

GUIDE TO THE GALAXY

D0808834

Smarties titles available

Smarties Beautiful Beasties
Smarties Book of Wizardry
Smarties Chuckle Factory
Smarties Deadly Dinosaurs
Smarties Dinosaurs Jokes
Smarties Guide to the Galaxy
Smarties Hairy Humans
Smarties Hilariously Funny Verse
Smarties How to Draw Cartoons
Smarties How To Make 'Em Laugh Joke Book
Smarties Joke Book
Smarties Knock Knock Jokes
Smarties Practical Jokes
Smarties Puzzle Busters
Smarties Smart Art
Smarties Smart Science
Smarties Travel Teasers
Smarties Wacky World
Smarties Wizard Jokes

GUIDE TO THE GALAXY

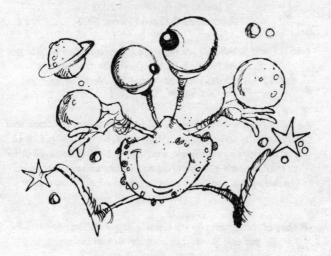

By Michael Powell

Illustrations by David Mostyn

Robinson Children's Books

First published in the UK by Robinson Children's Books,
an imprint of Constable & Robinson Ltd, 2002

Constable & Robinson Ltd
3 The Lanchesters
162 Fulham Palace Road
London W6 9ER
www.constablerobinson.com

A copy of the British Library Cataloguing in Publication Data for
this title is available from the British Library.

ISBN 1-84119-625-8

Printed and bound in the EU

10 9 8 7 6

Contents

Introduction   1

Space Camp   5
Blast Off!   25
Around the World in Ninety Minutes   49
Moon Mission   73
Sun Mission   95
The Solar System   111
Space Junk   127
Deep Space   149
To Infinity and Beyond   171

Answers   183

Introduction

Introduction

Welcome to the coolest and most exciting guide to the galaxy . . . in the galaxy!

If you've ever wondered how to . . .

BUILD A ROCKET...
TRAIN AS AN ASTRONAUT...
SURVIVE IN SPACE...
CATCH A COMET...
SPACE WALK...FLY TO
THE MOON...LAND ON
MARS ...TIME
TRAVEL AND
CROSS
GALAXIES...

...WITHOUT STARVING, EXPLODING,
FREEZING, BEING HIT BY AN ASTEROID,
EATEN BY AN UNFRIENDLY ALIEN
OR SUCKED INTO A BLACK HOLE...

Introduction

Chapter One
SPACE CAMP

SO YOU WANT TO FLY IN SPACE? WELL, IT'S GOING TO BE TOUGH. BUT IF YOU WANTED TO DO SOMETHING SIMPLE, YOU WOULDN'T WANT TO BE AN ASTRONAUT RIGHT?

FAILED

Top Guns

In the beginning you had to be a jet pilot and an engineering whizz to become an astronaut. Five hundred top guns were given tough physical and mental tests, but just seven were chosen as the first American astronauts.

Now NASA and the European Space Agency also accept applications from very bright and physically fit civilians. But you'll need a science degree or even a PhD!

Astronaut Test

Answer these questions to be selected for the space mission in chapter two. If you don't know the answers, read this chapter and try again.

1   Name four types of astronaut.
2   What does MMU stand for?
3   What is the Vomit Comet?
4   How many litres does an In-suit Drink Bag (IDB) contain?
5   Can you hear anything in space?
6   How many hours of jet experience must a pilot astronaut have?
7   What is a micrometeoroid?
8   Why do astronauts practise in swimming pools?
9   What is Dacron?
10 How much does an EMU weigh?

TOUGH QUESTIONS!
READ ON TO BEGIN YOUR
ASTRONAUT TRAINING
AND FIND
THE ANSWERS

Astronaut Types

There are four types of astronaut. Which one would you like to be?

COMMANDER
Big Boss. Responsible for safety of the craft and crew. Minimum 1,000 hours jet-pilot experience.

PILOT
Second in command. Minimum 1,000 hours jet-pilot experience.

MISSION SPECIALIST
Co-ordinates fuel, water, food, air supplies, conducts experiments and does space walks.

PAYLOAD SPECIALIST
Expert in operating very complicated and expensive Shuttle equipment.

Astronaut Training

The first lessons are about safety – THE most important part of any mission.

Trainee astronauts also learn maths, earth resources, meteorology, astronomy, physics and computer sciences. They learn about the Space Shuttle systems with lots of lectures, textbooks and manuals.

Nobody 'wings it' in space! Every part of a mission must be planned and practised using mock-ups and simulators – even eating, sleeping and going to the toilet. Everyone must be ready for every event that happens during a mission – especially when things go wrong.

Use The Force

Astronauts face enormous stress called G-Force when they speed up or slow down during take-off and landing. Without training the astronaut could black out.

If you've ever been on a roller coaster then you, too, have felt the force! G-Force pushes you back in your seat and makes your tummy feel weird.

Astronauts train in a 'centrifuge'. This is a capsule attached to a long arm which whizzes them around in a circle very fast. They experience up to 8g (8 times their body weight).

Gravity, What Gravity?

One of the biggest problems astronauts have to cope with is gravity: most training involves learning how to live in microgravity (very weak gravity). But what exactly is gravity?

Everything in the universe attracts everything else, like a magnet. The bigger something is, the more attraction or 'gravity' it exerts. Also the closer you are to something, the greater its attraction.

The only gravity we notice is between the Earth and everything else. That's the reason that things stay put and don't float into the air.

Gravity, What Gravity?

Space begins about 120km (75 miles) up in the air. But that's *not* the reason for microgravity in space. To completely escape the Earth's gravity you would have to travel 17 times further away than the Moon – about 6 million km!

Gravity, What Gravity?

Astronauts float in space because they are actually free falling, like skydivers. But a spacecraft can stay in orbit if it travels at the same speed as it is falling. If it travels too slowly it will fall back to earth; if it goes too fast it will shoot away.

Sims, Swims & Spins

NASA uses three ways to help astronauts on Earth get used to microgravity.

1. **Simulators:** the coolest computer games in the world!

2. **Neutral Buoyancy Lab (NBL):** a large swimming pool 61m (202ft) long, 31m (102ft) wide and 12m (40ft) deep. It holds 28 million litres (6.2 million gallons) of water. Astronauts wear little weights on their spacesuits to make them 'neutrally buoyant': they float suspended, like in space.

3. **The Vomit Comet:** This is a modified Boeing 707 aeroplane without seats – just a big empty shell with padded walls.

   The plane climbs steeply, then the engines are cut and the plane dives so quickly that everyone on board goes into free fall.

   The astronauts have just 40 seconds to practise eating and drinking and using various kinds of equipment. Gravity returns as the plane levels out and begins to climb again. Then it's time to hold on to your lunch for thirty more goes!

Astronaut Jokes

Why don't astronauts get hungry after being blasted into space?

Because they've just had a big launch.

Where do astronauts leave their spaceships?

At parking meteors.

What do astronauts wear to keep warm?

Apollo-neck jumpers.

Why is being an astronaut a strange job?

You have to be fired before you can work.

Space Clobber

Astronauts have more than one wardrobe. During take-off and re-entry they wear a partial pressure suit which stops blood collecting in the legs and making them pass out. In orbit inside the Space Shuttle astronauts wear 'normal' clothes (except that everything is flameproof!).

The answer is BOTH. There is no atmosphere in space to filter sunlight, so the side of your body that's facing the Sun may get as hot as 250°F, while your other side may reach −250°F.

So an astronaut could fry an egg on one side of his body while reaching for an ice cream from behind his back!

What, No Suit?

Unconscious within 15 seconds because there is no oxygen.

Tissues: skin, heart, liver and kidneys explode.

Blood and body fluids boil and then freeze because there is no air pressure.

Exposed to deadly radiation from the Sun and outer space.

Hit by hi-speed particles of dust or rock called micrometeoroids and other space junk.

What, No Suit?

SUITS MUST BE WORN AT ALL TIMES

Suits You

A spacesuit is also called an EMU (extravehicular mobility unit). It consists of many layers of tough fabric (Dacron or Kevlar) to protect against tearing and micrometeoroids.

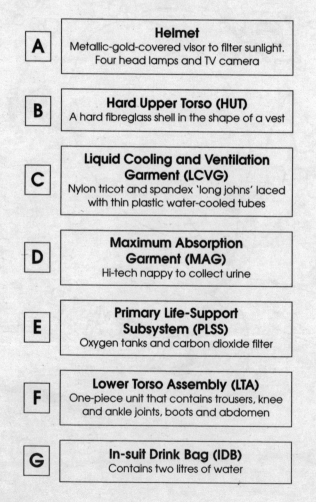

A **Helmet**
Metallic-gold-covered visor to filter sunlight.
Four head lamps and TV camera

B **Hard Upper Torso (HUT)**
A hard fibreglass shell in the shape of a vest

C **Liquid Cooling and Ventilation Garment (LCVG)**
Nylon tricot and spandex 'long johns' laced with thin plastic water-cooled tubes

D **Maximum Absorption Garment (MAG)**
Hi-tech nappy to collect urine

E **Primary Life-Support Subsystem (PLSS)**
Oxygen tanks and carbon dioxide filter

F **Lower Torso Assembly (LTA)**
One-piece unit that contains trousers, knee and ankle joints, boots and abdomen

G **In-suit Drink Bag (IDB)**
Contains two litres of water

Suits You

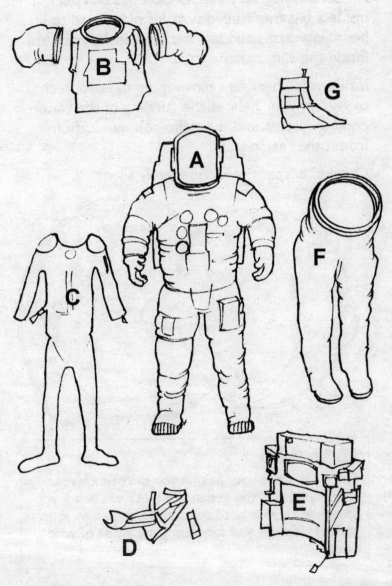

Inside an EMU

An EMU is not very comfortable. It's like being inside a big, overstuffed tyre. It's quite hard to bend your arms and legs because of the pressure inside the suit.

Inside you'll hear fans blowing air to keep fresh oxygen in your helmet, the gurgling of the water-cooling system, and the radio communication from other astronauts.

Outside in space, it is completely silent.

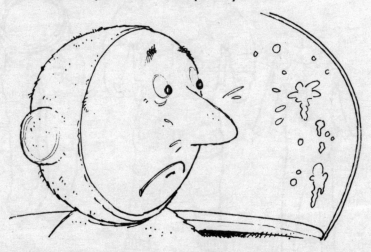

Survival Tip

Once you close your helmet you can't touch your face anymore. If you get an itch that's too bad. If you sneeze: tuck your head down and sneeze into your chest. This stops you splattering the inside of your visor!

Space Diving

Moving Around

An astronaut uses a MMU (manned manoeuvring unit) to move. This is a nitrogen-propelled backpack. The astronaut has a tether to stop him/her and tools from floating away. Astronauts also pull themselves along using handles bolted to the spaceship.

HE'S IN THERE SOMEWHERE!

Future Spacesuits

Thirty years ago the astronauts working on the Moon found moving about very difficult and tiring because their spacesuits were much less flexible than the EMU used today.

For future space missions to Mars, NASA is developing 'hard suits' that are more flexible, stronger, lighter and easier to put on than current spacesuits.

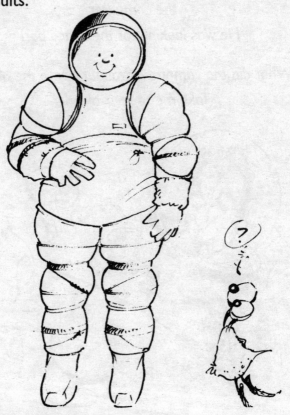

Astronaut Jokes

What's the difference between an astronaut
and a biscuit?

You can't dip an astronaut in your tea.

Why did the astronaut hold his boot to his ear?

Because he liked sole music!

Why was the thirsty astronaut hanging around
the computer?

He was looking for the space bar!

What did the vampire astronaut say to the aliens?

Take me to your bleeder.

Chapter Two
BLAST OFF!

Pulling Power

Because of the Earth's gravity it takes a lot of power and speed to get a spaceship off the ground: a rocket must travel faster than 11km per second (7 miles per second). This is the Earth's 'escape velocity'.

What Is A Rocket?

A rocket engine is a 'reaction' engine. The basic principle driving a rocket engine is Isaac Newton's law that 'to every action there is an equal and opposite reaction.'

Burning fuel forces gas out at very high speeds in one direction; the rocket has an equal reaction by shooting in the other direction!

If you blow up a balloon and let it go it flies all over the room: you have made a simple rocket engine. In this case, what is being forced out is the air inside the balloon.

WHAT CAN THAT PARPING BE?

UNCLE EDDIE IN ← A SPIN

Rocket History

300 BC The Chinese celebrate religious festivals by throwing bamboo tubes filled with saltpetre, sulphur and charcoal into ceremonial fires to frighten away evil spirits. Badly sealed ones become the first rockets, shooting out of the fire rather than exploding.

13th Century AD The Chinese use explosive grenades, cannons and huge rocket 'fire-arrows' (arrows powered by small gunpowder rockets) against their enemies. Europe and Arabia start to use them too.

AD 1500 Wan Hu ties rockets and kites to a chair and is fired into the air. He is never seen again! Was he the first man in space?

Rocket History

15th Century The Italians start using rockets for fun: fireworks!

18th Century Englishman Sir William Congreve invents barrage rockets weighing up to 135kg (300lb). This new-fangled technology is used against Napoleon!

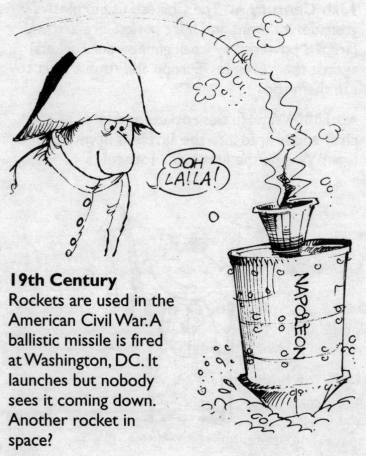

19th Century Rockets are used in the American Civil War. A ballistic missile is fired at Washington, DC. It launches but nobody sees it coming down. Another rocket in space?

Rocket History

1919 American Robert Goddard begins his experiments. He suggests a demonstration rocket should be sent to the Moon. Everyone thinks he's mad!

16 March 1926 Goddard launches the first liquid-powered rocket at his aunt's farm in Auburn, Massachusetts. It flies 46m (152ft)!

September 1944 Wernher von Braun's V2 rockets hit London. Fuelled by alcohol and liquid oxygen, they fly 80km (52 miles) high with a 320-km (200-mile) range. The Nazis' most deadly weapon in World War II.

1945 Von Braun and his team of rocket scientists begin working for the Americans instead. Russia and America compete to be the first to get into space. The Space Race begins.

Rocket History

1958 The National Aeronautics and Space Administration (NASA) is established in America.

31 January 1958 NASA launches America's first satellite, *Explorer I*.

12 April 1961 Russian Yuri Gagarin becomes the first man in space with a 108-minute flight.

5 May 1961 Alan Sheppard becomes the first American in space.

July 1969 Americans Buzz Aldrin and Neil Armstrong are the first men on the Moon.

14 May 1973 NASA's first experimental space station *Skylab* is launched to prove humans can live and work in space for long periods. It orbits for six years before crashing back to Earth in 1979.

12 April 1981 First Space Shuttle mission.

1994 Russia and America finally start working together with Shuttle *Mir* and the International Space Station.

2004 The International Space Station will be completed: the largest and most complex international scientific project in history.

GAME LINK

Play astropoop at
http://www.kosmonaut.se/gagarin/
index_game.html

Rocket Puzzle

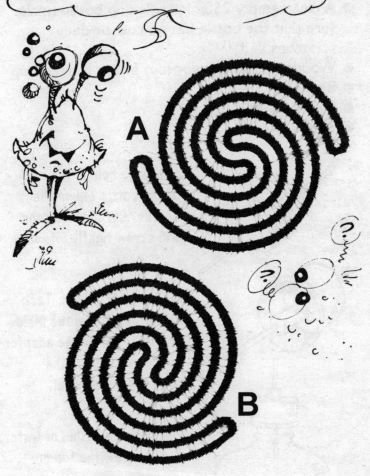

ONE OF THE TWO SPIRALS BELOW IS THE VAPOUR TRAIL OF ONE ROCKET.
THE OTHER SPIRAL WAS MADE BY TWO SEPARATE ROCKETS. CAN YOU SEE WHICH IS WHICH USING ONLY YOUR EYES?

A

B

Answer on page 183

Build A Rocket

Here's how to build your own rocket. Make sure you ask an adult to help throughout. All rockets are dangerous if handled wrongly.

You'll need
- A clean empty 250ml plastic pop bottle (make sure that the bottle has no cuts or deep scratches in it).
- Woods/Shrader adaptor (buy from a bicycle shop)
- Blu-Tack
- 140ml water
- Bicycle pump

1. Make a hole in the centre of the bottle top so the Woods/Shrader adaptor will screw tightly into it.

2. Place a ring of Blu-Tack around the hole on the inside of the top. Screw the adaptor through the hole so the Blu-Tack forms a seal.

3. Pour in 140ml of water and screw the top on.

Build A Rocket

4. Screw the bicycle pump pressure hose onto the adaptor.

5. Find a place well away from cars, people and buildings.

6. Invert the bottle and pump air into the bottle 12 times.

7. Quickly unscrew the bicycle pump hose from the adaptor while holding the bottle gently by the base of the neck, pointing upwards and well away from your face.

8. Lift off! The rocket should shoot about 10m into the air and you will get soaked with water!

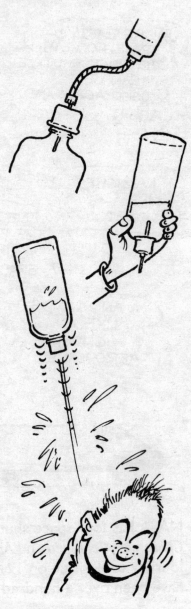

The Space Shuttle

NASA has four space shuttles named *Endeavour*, *Challenger*, *Columbia* and *Atlantis*. The first Shuttle journey took place on 12 April 1981 and there have been over a hundred missions since.

The Space Shuttle

The main challenge is that the shuttle needs LOTS of fuel. The orbiter (i.e. the bit you want to get into space) weighs 74,844kg (165,000lb) and can carry 29,250kg (65,000lb) of luggage (called the payload).

But the total weight including fuel and tanks is 2.05 million kg (4.5 million lb). So the fuel weighs nearly 20 times more than the orbiter!

The liquid fuel alone would fill the petrol tanks of 52,600 family cars! The 'solid' fuel (a thick, jelly-like mixture of resin and fuel) weighs the same as 16,000 children!

The Space Shuttle

Crew compartment
Pilot's seat and controls are upstairs and the galley (kitchen), sleeping and hygiene areas are downstairs.

Payload bay
Where payloads are carried into orbit, e.g. a satellite or parts of the International Space Station.

Solid rocket boosters (SRBs)
These are like huge fireworks that drop off after about 2 minutes and parachute into the ocean. A recovery team rescues them for the next mission.

Three main engines
Only fire during launch and ascent to orbit.

External fuel Tank (ET)
Supplies the main engines. Filled with hydrogen and oxygen.

Heat tiles protect against intense heat of re-entry.

COOL LINK
Visit the NASA Shuttle Countdown Information Centre at http://science.ksc.nasa.gov/shuttle/countdown/ for the countdown information on the latest mission.

The Space Shuttle

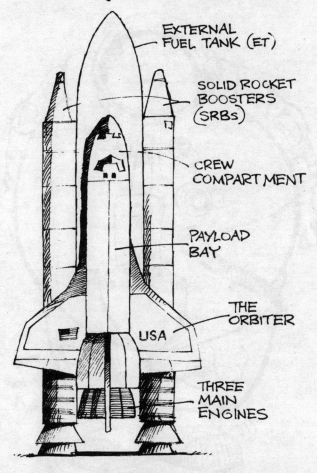

EXTERNAL FUEL TANK (ET)

SOLID ROCKET BOOSTERS (SRBs)

CREW COMPARTMENT

PAYLOAD BAY

THE ORBITER

USA

THREE MAIN ENGINES

A fuel (liquid hydrogen) and an oxidiser (liquid oxygen) are burned to create a high-pressure stream of hot gases. These gases whizz through a nozzle that speeds them up even more. The engine throws the gas out in one direction in order to get a reaction in the opposite direction. Lift off!

Weight Puzzle

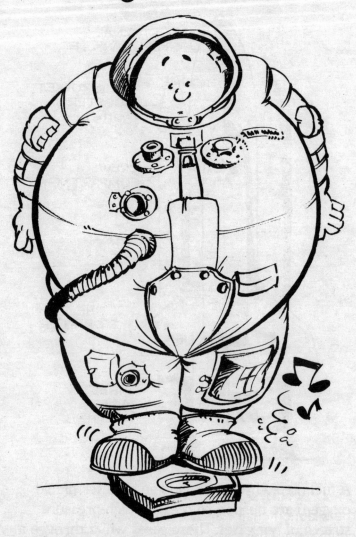

This astronaut weighs 64kg (142lb) plus half his own weight. How much does he weigh?
Answer on page 183

Countdown

HERE'S WHAT HAPPENS WHEN THE SHUTTLE LAUNCHES

FLIGHT DIRECTOR

T –3 Hours and holding The shuttle is fuelled up with liquid oxygen and hydrogen.

T –3 Hours The astronauts have been woken up, eaten breakfast and are wearing their 'Launch and Entry suits'. They take 20 minutes to travel to the launch pad.

T –2½ Hours The astronauts are strapped into their launch chairs, and begin checking their equipment. These are called 'Comm Checks'.

T –20 Minutes Everybody involved checks in to confirm whether they are 'Go' for launch.

Countdown

T –9 Minutes and holding
Any problems now and there's just 4 minutes to fix them otherwise the countdown must be called off before T –5.

GAME LINK

http://imedia.ksc.nasa.gov /shuttlesim/index.html for shuttle launch simulation.

T –5 Minutes 'Go to start APUs': the Auxiliary Power Units are activated and the shuttle is now on internal power.

T –31 seconds Ground Launch Sequencer (GLC) – the computer on the ground hands over control of the countdown to the on-board computers in the shuttle.

T –10 seconds Sparks are sprayed around the bottom of the shuttle to burn any extra hydrogen in the air (to prevent an explosion).

T –6.6 seconds The main engines ignite. The shuttle sways slightly (a phenomenon called 'twang'). As the shuttle sways back to the vertical it's ...

Lift-Off

T –0. LIFT-OFF

The Solid Rocket Boosters are ignited. Explosive bolts free the shuttle from the launch tower and it leaves the ground.

The countdown is now over. We begin counting in Mission Elapsed Time, MET.

Mission Elapsed Time

7 Seconds MET The shuttle clears the launch tower. Mission control switches from the Kennedy Space Center, to the Johnson Space Center in Houston Texas. The astronauts are now travelling 'uphill' (the understatement of the year!).

1 Minute MET Max-Q – As the shuttle goes through the sound barrier, the engines are briefly 'throttled down' as the shuttle crosses a kind of mid-air speed bump!

2 Minutes MET The Solid Rocket Boosters drop off and parachute into the ocean. Power now continues from the main engine.

4 Minutes MET If you're watching the launch without binoculars the shuttle will now be out sight.

8 Minutes MET MECO: Main Engine Cut-off. The shuttle is in space.

45 minutes MET The External Tank is jettisoned and burns up as it re-enters the Earth's atmosphere. The orbiter uses its Orbital Manoeuvring System engines to stabilise its orbit.

Future Rockets

Fuel powered rockets were invented over seventy years ago, but what will power the spaceships of the future? Here are four amazing ideas that actually work!

1. Magnets

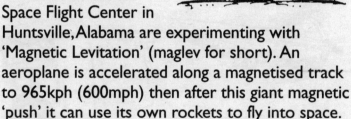

Soon rockets may be launched using electricity and magnets! Magnets are already being used on some modern trains and roller coasters. But scientists at NASA's Marshall Space Flight Center in Huntsville, Alabama are experimenting with 'Magnetic Levitation' (maglev for short). An aeroplane is accelerated along a magnetised track to 965kph (600mph) then after this giant magnetic 'push' it can use its own rockets to fly into space.

This launch method will be much cheaper. At the moment it costs tens of thousands of dollars to fuel the launch of the shuttle, but a maglev launch will use as little as $75 of electricity.

GAME LINK

http://www.spacekids.com/playanddo/playanddo/index.html

Future Rockets

2. Lasers

Riding laser beams into space sounds like a crazy idea but NASA and the US Air Force have already clocked up hundreds of successful test flights at the White Sands Missile Range in New Mexico. A powerful laser strikes the bottom of the Lightcraft which is lined with a thin coat of fuel. This detonates the fuel and pushes the Lightcraft into the air.

At the moment these little spaceships weigh only a few grams and are a few centimetres wide but as more powerful lasers are developed it will be possible to send bigger and bigger craft into space – and maybe one day, human beings!

ZAP!

COOL LINK
http://members.lycos.co.uk/ spaceprojects/propulsion.html

Future Rockets

3. Star Power

NASA is developing a plasma rocket, called the Variable Specific Impulse Magnetoplasma Rocket (VASIMR).

Plasma is the stuff that stars are made of. For real! It is electrically charged gas made up of special atoms which have bits missing!

A SPECIAL ATOM

↖ NOT THERE!

The VASIMR engine will actually create plasma from hydrogen then heat it even more using microwaves (like in a microwave oven). When the super-hot plasma shoots out of the rocket it delivers enormous thrust.

'Normal' rockets take about eight months to reach Mars, but a plasma spacecraft would only take three.

Future Rockets

4. Solar Sails

Four hundred years ago a scientist called Johannes Kepler imagined a spaceship with sails that could catch the 'solar wind' which he observed through his telescope blowing the tails of comets. Scientists today have discovered that sunlight does provide enough force to move objects.

When sunlight hits an object most is absorbed and some reflected. When it hits a mirror, much more is reflected and this creates a tiny thrust. However with an enormous mirror (or solar sail) it is possible to reflect enough sunlight to power a spaceship beyond the Solar System without fuel. By 2010, we may see solar sails being used for a long-distance NASA mission.

NASA is developing a solar sail that is nearly half a kilometre wide. Powered in this way a spaceship will start off moving slowly but with no air in space to slow it down the gentle push from the sunlight will make it go faster and faster until eventually it will reach speeds of over 320,000kph (200,000mph) – ten times faster than the Space Shuttle orbits the Earth. At this speed you could travel from London to New York in less than a minute.

Future Rockets

If NASA launches a probe powered by solar sails, it will take just eight years for it to catch the *Voyager 1* spacecraft which has been travelling for more than twenty. NASA is developing a laser or magnetic beam transmitter that could push a probe to a maximum speed of 30,000km/sec (18,600mi/sec) or one-tenth the speed of light. Soon you really will have the power to zip around the Solar System!

SEE CHAPTER EIGHT FOR SOME REALLY EXCITING WAYS OF TRAVELLING THROUGH SPACE!

A-LIEN

Rocket Jokes

Where do trained astronauts eat their lunch?
In the launch room.

Which knight fires a hundred rockets?
Sir Launchalot.

How do astronauts get their babies to sleep?
They rock-et.

Why did NASA send a pig into space?
Because they wanted the price of bacon to go up.

Chapter Three
AROUND THE WORLD IN NINETY MINUTES

International Space Station

This is being assembled 400km (250 miles) above your heads right now. This mammoth task involves 16 countries and is certain to be one of the greatest wonders of the modern world.

By 2004 it will have taken 45 launches and 1,705 hours of space walks to fit all the pieces of this monumental jigsaw together. It will have 70 major components and hundreds of minor ones.

The cost is astronomical: America's bill alone will be over $100 billion – nearly as much as all the Apollo moon missions put together.

International Space Station

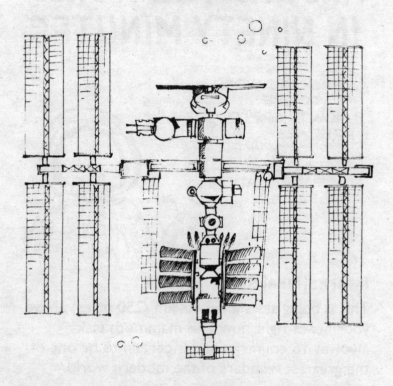

It will weigh more than 472,000kg (1,040,000lb) with living and working space equivalent to two Boeing 747s including six state-of-the-art laboratories.

An acre of solar panels will provide the power as it orbits the Earth once every 90 minutes (that's 16 times a day). The astronauts will see 16 sunrises and 16 sunsets every 24 hours!

International Space Station

Without gravity scientists can perform experiments that wouldn't be possible on Earth.

They hope to grow cells and create new chemicals to help us understand the building blocks of the universe and life itself.

They will make better and purer materials, for example metals for computer chips.

They will watch the Earth very carefully for, amongst other things, a study of the environment, weather and the effects of pollution.

Where is it?

Did you know that the ISS is visible with the naked eye? It looks like a dim star, but once finished it will be one of the brightest 'stars' in the sky.

COOL LINK

http://spaceflight.nasa.gov/realdata/tracking/index.html
A live map shows you the exact position of the ISS, so you know where in the sky to look.

Surviving In Space

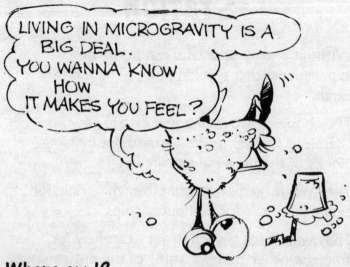

Where am I?

On Earth you usually find standing up quite easy!
Even with your eyes shut you can keep your
balance, thanks to special motion sensors in your
ears and pressure receptors in your muscles.

This system doesn't work well in microgravity.
You'll often feel upside down and it's even difficult
to know where your limbs are without looking!

Over half of all space travellers suffer from Space
Adaptation Syndrome: headaches, poor
concentration, feeling and being sick!

When you return to Earth you must adjust again:
you'll have problems balancing for a few days.

Surviving In Space

On Earth gravity pulls your blood and other fluids into the lower part of your body, but in space your legs shrink and more blood floats in to your upper body and head.

SPACEBATS DON'T HAVE THAT PROBLEM!

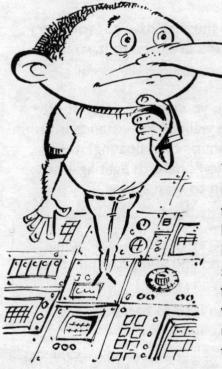

Your face will puff up and this extra fluid will give you a blocked nose. This is called the 'space sniffles'. It's like the feeling you get when you hang upside down for too long.

Surviving In Space

Veins in your legs contain tiny muscles that contract when the veins fill with blood. But in space, these muscles don't have to work as hard to keep your blood pressure balanced, so they get weaker. You will feel dizzy in space and may have blood pressure problems when you get home.

Astronauts drink lots of salt water to increase their body fluids and prevent dizziness. They also wear inflatable body suits (G-Suits), that squeeze arms and legs to balance their blood pressure.

On Earth bones and muscles have to work very hard against gravity. You are used to it, so it doesn't feel tough.

In space, even though you have to do a lot of physical work (space walking for instance is tiring – it's more like swimming than floating), your bones and muscles don't have to fight against gravity and they begin to waste away.

Good News: Microgravity allows your spinal vertebrae to expand and you grow up to 8cm (3in) taller.

Bad News: This can lead to backache and nerve problems.

Surviving In Space

On Earth new bone always grows to replace old bone. But in space old bone is not replaced because your body thinks your bones are on holiday and don't need it. You may lose up to 1 per cent of your bones each month.

Lazy Slobs!

NASA actually pays volunteers to lie in bed for weeks at a time so they can study bone and muscle wastage in space.

CAN'T GET UP IN THE MORNING?

Just want to lie in bed all day ... and the next day ... and the next?

Then the Bone and Mineral Laboratory at NASA wants *YOU*.

- We need volunteers to take part in our microgravity research into muscle and bone loss.

- We'll pay you to stay in bed for seventeen weeks. Don't delay! Get paid to be a lazy slob. Call us now (if you can be bothered to pick up the phone).

EXERCISE REDUCES MUSCLE WASTAGE AND GENERALLY IMPROVES ASTRONAUTS' SENSE OF WELL-BEING.
SO THEY COMPLETE AT LEAST TWO HOURS OF EXERCISE EACH DAY IN SPACE (ON A TREADMILL OR CYCLING MACHINE).

Solar Panels Puzzle

Three shuttles are launched into space with solar panels for the International Space Station. Once assembled there should be five squares each with nine solar panels. Which of the three shuttles is carrying the correct payload?

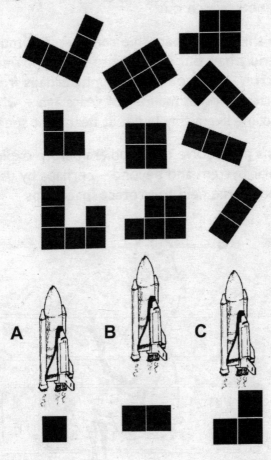

A B C

Answer on page 183

Radiation Warning

Harmful radiation continually whizzes around the Solar System: subatomic particles from the Sun (called 'solar wind') and from deep space. The Earth's atmosphere and magnetic field protect you, but further out in the Solar System, between the planets, watch out!

Even a thin metal spaceship can keep out much of this deadly hail. But it is hard to stop a powerful cosmic ray – an atomic fragment, perhaps from a star that exploded millions of years ago – when it is travelling like a tiny bullet at near light speed.

Humans must solve this problem before exploring the Solar System and beyond – perhaps by using a magnetic force field to protect spaceships.

Food and Drink

THIRTY-FIVE YEARS AGO SPACE FOOD FOR EARLY ASTRONAUTS WAS DEADLY DULL. IT WAS CUT INTO BITE-SIZED PIECES. FREEZE-DRIED TO A POWDER OR SERVED IN TUBES LIKE TOOTHPASTE. BORING.

Modern space food is much better but you will have to choose your menu well before you launch. Imagine deciding what you want to eat in three months' time!

Most of the shuttle foods are preserved by dehydration – like a Pot Noodle, you just add water (a by-product of the shuttle's fuel cells – yeucch!). Other food is heat treated or 'irradiated' (blasted with radiation) to kill germs. Finally 'free form' foods are just as on Earth – nuts, granola bars etc. (No bread: too many crumbs – tortillas are used instead.)

Ketchup, mustard, mayonnaise and other sauces are served in little sachets, just like in a café. Salt is dissolved in water and pepper in oil to avoid floating fragments.

Food and Drink

Select a bag pre-filled with powdered coffee, tea, milk or one of 17 other delicious beverages! Add hot or cold water then drink with a straw. The straw has a valve which closes between sips to avoid spills.

You may use a meal tray to hold your food packs. The tray can be attached to a wall or strapped to your lap.

You have been provided with your own set of cutlery: knife, fork, two spoons and a pair of scissors to open up the packages.

Empty containers should be thrown away in the waste compartment below the mid-deck floor; the cutlery must be carefully cleaned and sterilised with special wet wipes after use.

Food and Drink

SHUTTLE MENU

A typical daily menu on the shuttle or Space Station provides about 2,700 calories.

Breakfast
Orange drink, peaches, scrambled eggs, sausage, cocoa, tortilla

LUNCH
Cream of mushroom soup, ham and cheese sandwich, stewed tomatoes, banana

DINNER
Shrimp cocktail, beefsteak, broccoli au gratin, strawberries, pudding, cocoa

POLITE NOTICE: Please keep the dining area, the toilet, and sleeping area clean at all times. Germs breed quicker in a small weightless area like a spacecraft. All rubbish must be sealed in plastic bags.

Moving Around

You must push yourself carefully through the spacecraft, or else you will float around helplessly. And you must learn how to stop yourself, otherwise you'll keep on going!

Remember Newton's principle that to every action there is an equal and opposite reaction? This means that if you try to turn a screw without anchoring yourself to a wall, you will twist instead. The tiniest thing – even typing at a computer keyboard – will send you floating away. Anchor your feet in the restraining loops first.

You may, like many astronauts, choose to move around like a big baby in the 'foetal position' (curled up like a baby in its mother's womb) – it's comfortable and natural.

Space Puzzle

How can the astronaut stand behind the alien at the same time as the alien is standing behind the astronaut? (Time travel is not allowed.)

Answer on page 183

Sleeping

You need less sleep in space because your body does less work in a microgravity.

You are advised to sleep close to a ventilator fan. With no airflow you may find yourself waking up gasping for breath as the carbon dioxide that you breath out builds up around your face and suffocates you.

You should hook yourself to a wall. You may try floating freely, but don't be surprised if you wake up with your face in a ventilator grill!

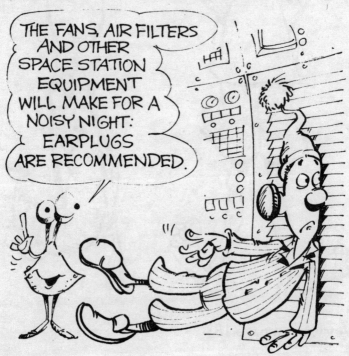

THE FANS, AIR FILTERS AND OTHER SPACE STATION EQUIPMENT WILL MAKE FOR A NOISY NIGHT: EARPLUGS ARE RECOMMENDED.

Space Walk Puzzle

These four symbols are printed on the bay pod doors. In order to open the doors you must trace your finger around the correct symbol without taking your finger off and without repeating yourself. This is possible on only one of these symbols. Which is it?

1

2

3

4

Answer on page 184

Shower

A shower is provided for your comfort and to prevent the spread of germs. Water squirts out of the 'top' and is sucked 'down' by an air fan in the floor. Please use water sparingly. (Astronauts today don't know they're born!)

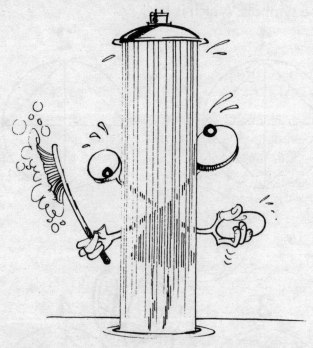

Dressing can be tricky when your limbs are floating around. Washing machines are not provided. Therefore please change trousers once a week and socks, shirts and underwear every other day. Please seal clothes in airtight plastic bags after use.

Toilet Trouble

Nobody allowed for going to the toilet when Alan Sheppard became the first American in space. The flight only took 15 minutes but he was stuck in his spacesuit lying on his back for hours before the launch and wet himself. Who said being an astronaut was glamorous?

NASA promptly designed a poop-bag which could be stuck on to your bottom. But there were still a few unpleasant moments in space history when poop escaped and had to be recaptured!

Fortunately the shuttle has a toilet. It cost $23.4 million to design and build, easily making it the most expensive loo in the galaxy.

Designing a toilet is easy on Earth, because gravity pulls waste down, away from you. But in space it kinda just floats around. That's why NASA came up with ...

Toilet Training

The Waste Collection System – WCS

Instructions for use

1. Remove trousers and underwear.

2. Fasten yourself to the toilet seat with spring-loaded restraining bars to ensure a good seal.

3. If the restraining bars malfunction, please use the backup system of a set of four Velcro thigh straps.

4. Place feet in the foot restraints.

5. You may stand or sit.

6. When the toilet is in use, you will hear a continuous flow of cabin air whistling in through holes under the seat. This will ensure that all waste is pulled to the bottom of the toilet (because there is no gravity).

7. 'Flush' by opening the valve. This exposes solid matter to the vacuum of space – where it is instantly freeze-dried. It will then be brought back to Earth for analysis!

8. The water waste travels to the waste water tank which is dumped into space.

9. Now wash your hands with sterile wipes.

10. Don't forget to put your underwear and trousers back on.

Animal Astronauts

HUMANS WERE'NT THE FIRST ANIMALS IN SPACE.

Laika ('Barker') the dog was the first living creature in space. She was launched aboard the *Sputnik 2* on 3 November 1957. She never returned to Earth but died in space about a week later.

Chimps Able and Baker were launched 300 miles high on 28 May 1959 in the nose cone of Jupiter Missile AM-18. They travelled at over 16,000 km/h (10,000mph) and returned safely. They were the first animals to survive a trip into space.

Two dogs Belka ('Squirrel') and Strelka ('Little Arrow') spent a day in orbit aboard *Sputnik 5* on 19 August 1960. They were joined by 40 mice, 2 rats and several plants. They returned safely and one of Strelka's puppies was later presented to President Kennedy.

Animal Astronauts

Ham was a 44-month-old chimpanzee who flew on board Mercury Capsule 5 at 11:55 am on 31 January 1961 and travelled at 9,425 km/h (5,857mph).

The first cat in space was a black and white tomcat called Felix on 18 October 1963.

An ark full of other animals has made it into space, including tortoises, rats, insects, quail eggs, fish, newts, frogs, mice and rats.

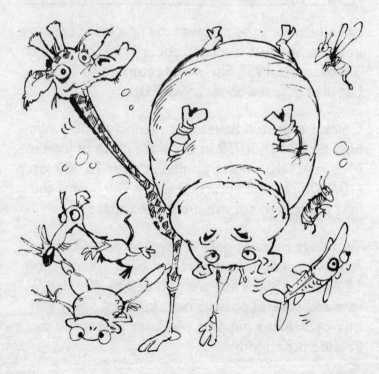

Space Tourism

So you want to be a space tourist? Have you ever dreamed of going to space and doing what only a few hundred people have done?

At the moment you need to be very rich if you want to go into space. Multi-millionaire Dennis Tito became the world's first space tourist aboard a Russian Soyuz rocket that arrived at the International Space Station on 30 April 2001. The trip cost him £14 million!

However, space tourism is set to become much cheaper within the next 20 years.

The Space Island Group plans to build a ring-shaped, rotating space hotel out of 12 empty NASA Space-Shuttle fuel tanks that are already in orbit. It will orbit 645km (400 miles) above the Earth and should be ready by 2006.

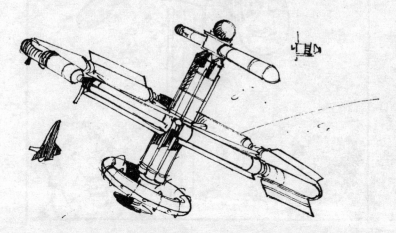

Jokes

Why did Albert Einstein install a knocker on his door?
He wanted to win the no-bell prize!

Doctor, Doctor I keep thinking I'm God
When did this start?
Well, first I created the Sun, then the Earth ...

How do we know that the Earth won't come
to an end?
Because it's round!

Why are astronauts successful people?
Because they always go up in the world!

Chapter Four
MOON MISSION

FULL EARTH TONIGHT!

It's staggering to think that everybody who has ever lived has looked up at the same moon that now circles the Earth 363,284km (225,745 miles) away. As the Earth's only natural satellite and the second brightest object in the sky after the Sun, it has always filled humans with wonder.

But how much do you know about the Moon? Do you know how it was made? What exactly is a blue moon? And what is moon dust's proper name?

Old Moon

The Moon is about 4 billion years old and it's never far from your thoughts. People have prayed to it, howled at it and written about it for thousands of years. Only in the last 40 years have 12 lucky men been able to visit and bring back pieces of this strange world.

When astronomer Galileo peered through his own handmade telescope in 1609 he created a storm by suggesting that the Moon was like the Earth – irregular with mountains, craters and valleys.

Astronomers in the 1880s thought they could see houses and oceans on the Moon. But it wasn't until the 20th century that humans understood the real truth. (The Moon was first visited by the Soviet spacecraft *Luna 2* in 1959.)

Making Waves

You may know that the Moon causes the tides in the ocean. But why? The gravitational pull from the Moon is greatest on the side of Earth that is closest. This actually pulls the ocean towards it causing a bulge. But because the Earth rotates much faster than the Moon moves in its orbit, the bulges move around the Earth about once a day giving two high tides per day.

COOL LINK

Map of the Moon at http://www.space.com/images/skywatchers_moon_map.gif

Moon Ice

The Moon has no atmosphere but there is water ice at both poles. So future moon colonies will have a water supply! Much cheaper than lugging it from Earth.

WATER, PLEASE.

How often is once in a blue moon?

A blue moon occurs once every 2.7 years. It is when two full moons occur in the same calendar month.

Cool Moon Facts

The Moon is actually moving away from Earth at a rate of 3.8cm (1.5in) each year. When it was formed, it was about 22,530km (14,000 miles) away. It's now more than 450,000km (280,000 miles) away.

The Moon is slowing the Earth down – but don't panic. It's only by about 1.5 milliseconds every hundred years.

The footprints left by the Apollo astronauts will last at least 10 million years because there is no wind or water on the Moon to rub them away.

When walking on the Moon, astronaut Alan Sheppard hit a golf ball 730m (2,400ft).

Man in the Moon

When you look at the Moon you see a bright disk with dark splotches which seem to form a face. The bright areas are the ancient crust leftover from when the Moon was made. The dark patches (called *maria*, Latin for 'seas') are newer rock formed from volcanic eruptions. The Maya and Aztecs of ancient Mexico thought the 'face' looked like a rabbit.

You can always see the man in the moon because the Moon rotates synchronously. That means it is locked in phase with its orbit so that the same side is always facing toward the Earth.

YOO-HOO!

Moon Trick

Why does the Moon look bigger near the horizon?

Have you seen one of those enormous yellow moons? It isn't because the Moon is closer to us at certain times (though this is true). It's actually an optical illusion which was explained by Mario Ponzo in 1913.

Which of the two grey lines is the longer?

They are actually the same length, but the upper line appears longer because it seems to span a greater width of track.

If you look at a big Moon through a toilet roll tube it will appear small again because your brain can no longer compare it to the size of the trees and houses on the horizon.

Moon Trees

In 1971 astronaut Stuart Roosa took hundreds of seeds with him aboard *Apollo 14* which were planted when the mission returned to Earth. There are now over 400 'moon trees' scattered around the USA: Loblolly Pine, Sycamore, Sweetgum, Redwood and Douglas Fir.

Are there two moons?

For the next 5,000 years the Earth will have another 'moon'! How can that be? In 1999, scientists discovered a 5-km (3-mile) wide asteroid caught in Earth's gravitational field. It's called Cruithne and orbits the Earth in a horseshoe-shaped orbit every 770 years.

More Cool Moon Facts

The proper name for moon dust is regolith.

In 1988 an American survey discovered that 13% of the population believe that some part of the Moon is made of cheese.

The average desktop computer contains 10 times more computing power than was used to land men on the moon in 1969.

Bailly, the largest crater on the Moon is three times the size of Wales.

Moon Jokes

Which side of the Moon is the darkest?
The inside.

Why is a moon rock tastier than an Earth rock?
Because it is a little meatier (meteor).

What holds the Moon up?
Moon beams!

Why are parties on the Moon boring?
Because there's no atmosphere.

Where do moon people go after they get married?
On their honeyearth.

The Apollo 11 Story

On 16 July 1969 at 9:32 am, sitting in the small Command Module on top of *Saturn V* – the most powerful rocket ever built – three men were blasted into a clear blue sky at Cape Kennedy in Florida, USA. The spacecraft was *Apollo 11*. The three men were Neil Armstrong , Edwin Aldrin Jr (Buzz) and Michael Collins. Their mission was to land on the Moon and return safely to Earth.

They were all experienced pilots who had been in space on earlier missions, but they all knew that they and their thousands of support staff were creating history. Despite many years of preparation it was by no means certain that they would be successful.

The Apollo 11 Story

In December 1968 three astronauts in *Apollo 8* had circled the Moon ten times and returned safely. In March 1969 another three astronauts had practised docking the Lunar Module with the Command Module and in May 1969 two men left *Apollo 10* and rehearsed the lunar landing, descending to 16km (10 miles) above the surface of the Moon.

Then while thousands of people watched along the beaches of Florida and millions sat in front of their TV sets, it was time to keep the promise that President Kennedy made, way back on 25 May 1961 that America would land a man on the Moon by the end of the decade.

The Apollo 11 Story

Eleven minutes after lift-off the astronauts were in orbit around the Earth. Here they separated the Command Module from the third stage of the Saturn rocket, turned and docked with the Lunar Module (The Eagle). This was a critical time. Failure at this point would mean return to Earth. Docking was a success and they headed on to the Moon – a four-day journey of 450,000km (280,000 miles).

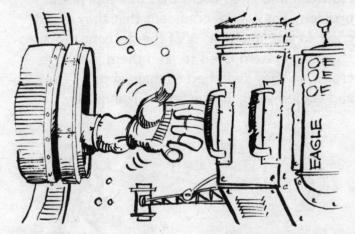

On the morning of the fifth day in orbit around the Moon, Buzz Aldrin and Neil Armstrong transferred into the Lunar Module (The Eagle). Michael Collins remained in orbit around the Moon in the Command Module.

COOL LINK

http://www.ksc.
nasa.gov/history/
apollo/apollo-
11/apollo-
11.html

The Apollo 11 Story

They were still 100km (60 miles) above the surface when they began their first 'burn' – a slight blast of their engine to change their orbit and begin the 12-minute descent.

When they were 1,800m (6,000ft) above the surface the astronauts received a yellow caution light – the computers were overloading. But Houston informed them that this was not a problem. They were confident that they could cope. In the final phases of the descent the auto-targeting system tried to land them in a huge crater, so they switched to manual to fly over it and landed safely in the Sea of Tranquillity.

The Apollo 11 Story

The dust settled immediately and they saw a landscape pockmarked with craters. There were lots of rocks of all shapes and sizes. Two hours later Neil Armstrong opened the hatch, backed out of the tiny door and said the famous words:

Fifteen minutes later Buzz joined him. He had goose pimples when he stepped down on the surface. He stared at his feet and noticed the sand scattering away exactly and precisely as he took his next step. Even though he weighed 163kg (360lb) with his spacesuit, here on the Moon he weighed one sixth of this. He began to jog. It was a strange feeling – like running in slow motion or in a dream.

The Apollo 11 Story

Buzz watched the stark shadows against the bright sand and then looked back at the Lunar Module, shining in this bleak brown landscape. Neil looked dazzling in his white spacesuit. It took both of them to set up the American flag – the pole wouldn't go far enough into the rocky ground. What a disaster it would be if the flag fell over in full view of millions.

Then President Nixon spoke to Neil and Buzz live and congratulated them, speaking about bringing peace and tranquillity to the Earth. They left a plaque saying 'HERE MEN FROM PLANET EARTH FIRST SET FOOT UPON THE MOON. JULY 1969 AD. WE CAME IN PEACE FOR ALL MANKIND.'

The Apollo 11 Story

They collected 21kg (46lb) of soil samples, took photographs, and set up some scientific experiments then returned to the Lunar Module to rest for several hours. After a lunar surface stay of 21.6 hours they returned to the orbiting Command Module.

Space Junk

That wasn't all they left. In addition to the flag and the plaque they jettisoned boots, backpacks, empty food packets, and used urine bags. The gold-plated 33-rpm record *Camelot* was also left behind.

The Apollo 11 Story

Then they headed back to Earth, splashing down in the Pacific Ocean on 24 July.

What's the best way to travel to the Moon?

Walking (at 4mph)	2351 days (6.4 years)
Marathon runner (13mph)	723 days (nearly 2 years)
Bicycle (25mph)	376 days
Car (70mph)	135 days
Train	forget it!
Concorde (1,336mph)	7 days
Rocket	4 days

Moon Puzzle

```
C A N U F N F Z A D H B X F P
H T D H F O L C M V J U A N C
E K R E G O L I T H T H D W Y
E Y C A T M O S P H E R E O U
S F C R N Y C R A T E R L D D
E Q P M E Q D N O T S U O H V
F C W S I Z U E O J I W P S Y
N O C T L C Z I N E S U A A A
I M O R C O H U L N L T N L T
R M L O I L M A B L E I U P N
D A L N A L C J E L I K L S P
L N O G I I J O L L U T Z A R
A D P I S N R I J G L E Y W G
Z G A M N S T A W Q J M M X D
K E L G A E U Q M O D U L E R
```

Can you find these moon words?

ALDRIN	COMMAND	MICHAEL
APOLLO	CRATER	MODULE
ARMSTRONG	EAGLE	MOON
ATMOSPHERE	GALILEO	NEIL
BLUE	HOUSTON	REGOLITH
BUZZ	KENNEDY	SATELLITE
CHEESE	LUNA	SPLASHDOWN
COLLINS	MARIA	TRANQUILLITY

Answer on page 184

Was It A Hoax?

Some people doubt NASA had the technology to make it to the Moon. They believe that there was so much pressure on America to keep Kennedy's promise to

COOL LINK

http://www.webaxs.net/~noel/moon.htm for lots of great moon hoax theories

put a man on the Moon by the end of the sixties and beat the Russians, that NASA asked Stanley Kubrick (who directed *2001: A Space Odyssey*) to fake it in a top-secret TV studio in the Nevada desert.

Consider these questions, then look at the explanation.

1. WHY AREN'T THERE ANY STARS IN THE PHOTOGRAPHS?

2. WHY DID THE FLAG RIPPLE AS IF IN A BREEZE?

3. IF NEIL ARMSTRONG WAS THE FIRST MAN ON THE MOON, WHO FILMED HIM COMING OUT OF THE LUNAR MODULE?

Was It A Hoax?

So, it seems like the whole thing was faked ... until you read these simple answers:

COOL LINK
http://www.redzero.demon.co.uk/moonhoax/ to see why these hoax theories are rubbish.

1. THE LUNAR SURFACE IS VERY BRIGHT. THE CAMERAS WERE SET TO 'BRIGHT.' SO THE STARS WERE TOO DIM TO SHOW UP.

2. THERE WAS A VIDEO CAMERA ON THE SIDE OF THE LUNAR MODULE.

3. PLANTING THE FLAG MADE IT RIPPLE. BUT IT CONTINUED BECAUSE THERE WAS NO ATMOSPHERE TO MAKE IT STOP.

Moon Jokes

What do you call a mad person on the Moon?
A luna-tic.

What became of the man who was swallowed by
a cow?
He became the man in the moo.

When can't you land on the Moon?
When it's full!

What's the fastest way to get to the Moon?
Climb into an elephant's trunk and tickle him.

Chapter Five
SUN MISSION

What's the best way to travel to the Sun?

Walking (at 4mph)	2,654 years
Marathon runner (13mph)	816 years
Bicycle (25mph)	424 years
Car (70mph)	151 years
Train	Forget it!
Concorde (1,336mph)	7.9 years
Rocket	4.5 years (about 1650 days)

A Star is Born

The Sun began to form about 4.6 billion years ago when a swirling cloud of dust and gas called the accretion disk started collapsing. The leftovers became the planets (see page 111).

The Sun is a star – and although it is a pretty average star it's the only one you've got! (Many of the stars in the sky are much bigger than the Sun, but they are so far away they look tiny.) It's the power source that drives the Solar System while its enormous gravity keeps all the planets in its orbit.

Hot Stuff

The Sun's energy is created when hydrogen atoms fuse to make helium. This is called nuclear fusion. The Sun 'uses up' 4 million tons of hydrogen in this way every second to produce an estimated 386 billion, billion megawatts. That's the same amount of energy in 15 minutes that everyone on Earth uses all year! And it's still got enough fuel to keep it burning away for another 5 billion years.

Sun Jokes

Which is more useful, the Sun or the Moon?

The Moon: it shines at night, when it is dark; the Sun shines during the day when it's already light!

Why does the Sun shine brighter on Saturdays and Sundays?

Because all the other days are weak days.

What sort of spots can't you squeeze?

Sun spots.

What's the definition of useless?

A solar-powered torch!

How Big?

Average it may be compared to other stars, but the Sun is huge! The Earth is minuscule in comparison. If the Sun were a basketball, the Earth would be the size of a pinhead.

It's also a very long way away – 150 million km (93 million miles). If you placed your basketball Sun on the goal line of a football pitch, the pinhead would be 30.5 metres (100ft) away. If a person had started walking to the Sun 650 years before the birth of Jesus, he would be arriving just about now! Even the light from the Sun travelling at 299,792,458 metres per second takes 8.3 minutes to reach us.

GADZOOKS !! A HORSELESS HORSE !!

What If . . . I took the car? You would have had to start driving in the 1850s – 50 years before cars were even invented.

Sun Spots

All the gas in the Sun spins around its axis but between the poles and the equator the gas travels at different speeds with amazing results: over a period of 22 years the Sun's magnetic poles actually swap places and back again. The Sun shows the most sun spots while the poles are changing.

These changes in the Sun's magnetic field also cause huge jets or loops of stellar material to shoot into space like a huge flame thrower. These are called solar flares.

The Sun weighs about 2 trillion, trillion, trillion tons; if it were possible to clump all the planets together, the Sun's mass would still be 750 times larger.

Big Star, Little Star

Here are two solar systems. The first star has eight planets and the second has only five. But which is the bigger star?

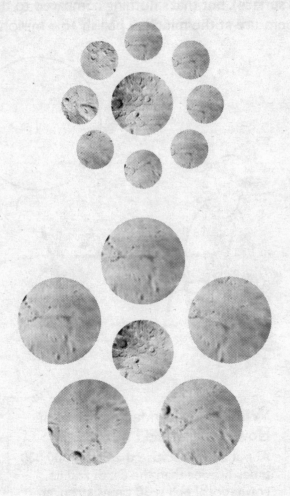

Answer on page 184

Crash Landing

'Landing' on the Sun would be impossible even for a spaceship with state-of-the-art heat shields. The surface temperature is 5500°C (and it's not a solid surface). But that's nothing compared to the temperature at the middle: a hellish 15.6 million °C.

What if . . . I landed on the Sun? How much would I weigh?

About a ton, because the Sun is 300,000 times heavier than the Earth and its gravitational pull is 30 times stronger.

Old Shiner

The Sun is also much older than humans. It is about 4.5 billion years old. If you think of that as the length of a soccer pitch then humans have lived for less than the width of the goal line. The Sun is middle aged, nearly halfway through its life, and will burn its hydrogen until it runs out in about 5 billion years.

Old Shiner

Then the temperature at its core will increase as it switches to burning helium making the Sun grow about 100 times bigger and become a 'red giant'.

It will swallow up Mercury and make the oceans on Earth boil away.

Finally, about a thousand years later it will have shrunk again to become a small 'white dwarf', a dying star glowing like the embers of a fire (although its surface temperature will be about 20 times hotter than it is now).

Light Speed

Jane switches off the light in her bedroom. The light switch is 5 metres from her bed, but she still gets into bed before it is dark. How does she do it?

Answer on page 184

Light Show

The Sun gives a dazzling light show called the aurorae. These are colourful clouds of light that can be seen at night above the Earth's poles. This light moves around and changes colour in a dazzling dance.

The aurorae are caused by energetic particles coming from the Sun. Every once in a while the Sun can suddenly eject material – a million tons of it – into space. Some of this comes towards the Earth.

When it reacts with gas in the atmosphere light is released and appears in many different colours (green, blue and red).

In the north it is called aurora borealis, or northern lights. In the south it is called aurora australis, or southern lights.

What . . . No Sun?

What would you do without the Sun? If the Sun suddenly vanished, the Earth and all the other planets would instantly be catapulted into space. (It's the same as if you were spinning a conker on a string and then cut the string – the conker would fly off. The gravitational pull of the Sun is like the string.)

However it wouldn't go dark and cold until 8.3 minutes later, because the light takes this long to reach us. (Imagine a very powerful hose. When you switch off the tap the water stops but there is still a stream of water travelling in the air.)

Humans would all die and the Earth would hurtle through space for hundreds of thousands of years until finally it would get sucked into the orbit of another star.

Solar Eclipse

Sometimes the Moon passes between Earth and the Sun, blocking some or all of the sunlight. When it blocks some of the Sun we call it a partial eclipse. When it blocks all of the Sun it is called a total eclipse. During a total eclipse the outer atmosphere of the Sun, or corona, becomes visible.

A total eclipse of the sun is only visible from the same spot on Earth every 360 years, but happens somewhere on Earth about once a year.

CORONA

MOON

Survival Tip

NEVER look directly at the Sun with the naked eye nor with any optical device. The only safe way to observe the Sun is with a pinhole camera, or to project its image onto a piece of white paper using binoculars or a small telescope.

Solar Eclipse

Across the centuries, it has been considered as an evil or a bad omen.

On 28 May 585 BC a solar eclipse actually ended a five-year war between two ancient Middle Eastern nations. The Lydians and the Medes were so amazed by what they saw as a divine warning that they immediately agreed a peace treaty.

Sunny Jokes

What has a head and a foot but no arms?
A sun bed.

What washes up on very small beaches?
Microwaves!

What's black and white and red all over.
A zebra with sunburn.

Why did the idiot have his sundial floodlit?
So he could tell the time at night!

IT'S THREE MINUTES PAST MIDNIGHT!

Chapter Six
THE SOLAR SYSTEM

When the Sun began to form about 4.6 billion years ago from a swirling cloud of dust and gas, about 1 per cent of leftovers started forming solid lumps which collided with others to form bigger lumps until they eventually became protoplanets. These took millions of years to cool down and form the nine planets we know today.

COOL LINK
For 3D tour of the Solar System visit http://www.bbc.co.uk/science/space/solar system/3d_tour.shtml

Mercury

Named after: Roman messenger of the gods
Colour: Brown
1 Day = 58.65 Earth days
1 Year = 87.9 Earth days
High Temp: 430°C
Low Temp: −210°C
Minimum distance from Earth: 45 million km
Escape Velocity: 4.3 km/s
Your Weight: x0.3
Your Age: x4.15

Weather: As the planet closest to the Sun, it is the sunniest planet in the Solar System (but the hottest is Venus). Daytime temperatures reach 430°C but night-time temperatures sink to −210°C.

Traveller's Tips: Landing on it is quite easy, since it has little atmosphere. The air is mostly helium with a little hydrogen. Wear a spacesuit that protects you against both the heat and the cold.

Must see: It has lots of craters, just like the Moon.

There are enormous cliffs several hundred km long and up to 5km (3 miles) high.

Visit one of the largest impact craters in the Solar System. The Caloris Basin is 1,300km (800 miles) wide, with an area greater than the British Isles!

Mercury

Mercury rotates around its axis every two orbits around the Sun. A year is less than two Mercurian days, so you'd have a birthday every other day!

Mercury is quite similar in composition to the Moon. Some scientists think a major catastrophic impact during Mercury's early history might have deprived it of most of its rocks.

Past and Future Visits

The only spacecraft to ever visit Mercury was *Mariner 10* in 1974–5, which took about 10,000 photographs.

Venus

Named after: Roman goddess of beauty
Colour: Reddish brown
I Day = 243 Earth days
I Year = 225 Earth days
High Temp: 482°C
Low Temp: 446°C
**Minimum distance
from Earth:**
40 million km
Escape Velocity:
10.36 km/s
Your Weight: x0.9
Your Age: x1.62

Weather: This is the hottest planet in the Solar System – hot enough to melt lead. There is constant sulphuric acid rain and permanent thunderstorms. In the upper atmosphere there are 350km/h (215mph) winds. On the surface, because of the air pressure, the wind will sweep you away like a fast-flowing river!

Traveller's Tips: Venus will appear bright as you approach. But if you don't overheat in the dense atmosphere, on the rocky, barren surface the sky overhead will be quite dark as only about 2 per cent of the sunlight gets through the clouds.

However, the heat and the surface pressure will destroy you and your spaceship within minutes!

Venus

Must see: Active volcanoes a hundred kilometres wide and five kilometres high.

ISHTAR TERRA - A MOUNTAIN RANGE THE SIZE OF THE USA AND 12 km (7·5 MILES) HIGH.

Past and Future Visits

There have been many missions including *Venera 7*, the first spacecraft to land on another planet on 15 Dec 1970. Also Mariner, Pioneer and Magellan missions.

Mars

Named after: Roman god of war
Colour: Red
1 Day = 24.62 Earth hours
1 Year = 687 Earth days
High Temp: 27°C
Low Temp: −126°C
Minimum distance from Earth: 56 million km
Escape Velocity: 5.03 km/s
Your Weight: x0.3
Your Age: x0.53

Weather: The summer can be 27°C but storms can spring up with little warning, plunging the temperature down. Watch out for dust storms lasting months and tornadoes 8km (5 miles) high. Winter temperatures reach −133°C. No need to worry about the rainy season – it never rains. It is a desert much like Antarctica on Earth.

Traveller's Tips: You'll find Mars to be more like Earth than any of the other planets. But it is still a nightmare for space travellers.

Breathing is a big problem, since the atmosphere is 95.3 per cent carbon dioxide with very little oxygen. The air pressure is about 140th that on Earth – so take oxygen and a pressure suit unless you want to explode.

Mars

Must See: Mars has some of the largest volcanoes in the Solar System. The volcano Olympus Mons is the highest mountain in the Solar System – 25km (15 miles).

THAT'S NEARLY THREE TIMES THE HEIGHT OF MOUNT EVEREST.

Mars has two very different halves. The southern hemisphere is higher and more rugged, while the smoother northern hemisphere is about five kilometres lower.

GAME LINK
Mars Adventure
http://spaceplace.jpl.nasa.gov/mars_rocket.htm

Mars

The northern hemisphere has fewer impact craters, so it must be much younger than the southern hemisphere.

COOL LINK

http://science.nasa.gov/headlines/y2001/ast24may_1.htm

Mars also has polar ice caps made of frozen carbon dioxide.

In the sky you can see two moons, Phobos (Fear) and Deimos (Panic) which are probably captured asteroids.

Visit the Cydonia region and check out the Face. This is an unusual rock formation discovered by the *Viking Orbiter 1* in 1976. With the Sun at the correct angle these rocks look like a face and some believe it is an Egyptian Pharaoh made by aliens.

Past and Future Visits

In 1971 the US space probe, *Mariner 9*, orbited Mars and sent back images of this dry, barren, lifeless world. Again in 1976 *Viking 1* and 2 orbited and landed. The surface has been mapped by *Mars Global Surveyor*, and *Mars Pathfinder* landed in 1997.

Jupiter

Named after: Roman king of the gods
Colour: Orange
1 Day = 9.84 Earth hours
1 Year = 11.86 Earth years
High Temp: −118°C
Low Temp: −129°C
**Minimum distance
from Earth:**
588 million km
Escape Velocity:
59.5 km/s
Your Weight: x2.3
Your Age: x0.084

Weather: There are constant storms across the whole planet with bolts of lightning that could vaporise a whole city.

Traveller's Tips: Expect an 18-month trip to reach this gas giant. It is bigger than the other eight planets put together.

Your ship will need protection against the high energy radiation trapped within the planet's enormous magnetic field. It will kill any human tens of thousands of km away.

As you approach you'll get a spectacular view of its 16 moons and the bright colours of its atmosphere. Don't be tempted to land, because it's not solid, only gas and liquid hydrogen.

Jupiter

Must see: The Great Red Spot is the planet's star attraction and can even be seen from the Earth. It is a huge thunderstorm twice the size of Earth.

IT'S BEEN RAGING FOR AT LEAST 300 YEARS!

Past and Future Visits

Only the *Galileo* probe in 1995. It was crushed by atmospheric pressure 50 minutes after landing.

Saturn

Named after: Roman god of agriculture
Colour: Yellow
1 Day = 10.65 Earth hours
1 Year = 29.5 Earth years
High Temp: −179°C
Low Temp: −184°C
**Minimum distance
from Earth:**
1.2 billion km
Escape Velocity:
35.5 km/s
Your Weight: x0.9
Your Age: x0.034

Weather: Expect wind speeds of over 1500km/h (930mph) at the equator. Don't bother with a hat!

Traveller's Tips: After a journey from Earth of four years, this spectacular planet is well worth the trip. It is the next largest planet in the Solar System after Jupiter (755 times larger than the Earth).

Watch out for at least 18 moons as you approach and use your ship's ultra-violet viewfinder to see the aurora formed as particles collide with the atmosphere.

Like Jupiter, this is a gas giant and of similar composition, so don't bother trying to land on the 'surface'.

Saturn

Must see: Saturn has a spectacular ring system made of billions of small icy and rocky particles, from around 1cm to 5 metres (0.4in to 16ft) in size. These are probably pieces of comets or asteroids and there are a few larger objects as well.

THE RINGS ARE ONLY ABOUT 200M. (650 ft) THICK!

Past and Future Visits

Three NASA spacecraft, *Pioneer 11*, *Voyager 1* and *Voyager 2*, flew past Saturn in 1979–81, but none has visited since then. The Cassini mission was launched in 1997. It will arrive at Saturn in 2004, and send a probe to land on Saturn's largest moon, Titan.

Uranus

Named after: Greek god of the heavens
Colour: Bluish green
I **Day** = 17.23 Earth hours
I **Year** = 84 Earth years
High Temp: −208°C
Low Temp: −212°C
**Minimum distance
from Earth:**
2.57 billion km
Escape Velocity:
21.3 km/s
Your Weight: x0.8
Your Age: x0.012

Weather: There's not much visible weather except for the 1,000km/h (620mph) winds.

Traveller's Tips: It will take you 8.5 years to reach from Earth. Discovered in 1781 by Wilhelm Herschel who originally named it 'Georgium Sidus' (the Georgian Planet – after the king), it was later renamed Uranus.

Uranus spins on its side! And it takes 84 years to orbit the Sun – that means a year takes a lifetime!

Must See: This is another gas giant with rings and at least 15 moons. The methane in the atmosphere gives it a blue colour. It also has 11 dark rings.

Past and Future Visits

Only *Voyager 2* has visited Uranus, in 1986.

Neptune

Named after: Roman god of the sea
Colour: Blue
1 Day = 16.11 Earth hours
1 Year = 165 Earth years
High Temp: −209°C
Low Temp: −213°C
**Minimum distance
from Earth:**
4.3 billion km
Escape Velocity:
23.5 km/s
Your Weight: ×1.1
Your Age: ×0.006

Weather: The fastest winds in the Solar System reach speeds of 2,400km/h (1500mph). It has a large storm cloud called the Great Dark Spot.

Traveller's Tips: Expect a 12-year journey. Look out for eight moons and four very faint rings.

Must See: A small dark cloud (named 'Scooters') shoots around the planet every 16 hours.

Past and Future Visits

Voyager 2 flew over the north pole in 1989. It spotted active geysers on moon Triton which are thought to be burps of gaseous nitrogen on a world with the coldest known land temperature in the Solar System of −235°C.

Pluto

Named after: Greek god of the underworld
Colour: Blue
1 Day = 6.39 Earth days
1 Year = 247.7 Earth years
High Temp: −219°C
Low Temp: −220°C
Minimum distance from Earth: 4.34 billion km
Escape Velocity: 1.1 km/s
Your Weight: x0.6
Your Age: x0.004

Weather: The coldest planet in the Solar System. During winter, even the atmosphere freezes!

Traveller's Tips: Pluto is the furthest planet from the Sun – except for 20 years in every orbit, when it comes closer to the Sun than Neptune. Time your journey right and it will only take you eight years to reach. It even takes light 6.70 hours to reach Pluto.

Must See: Check out the Sun – it is so far away that it will just look like a bright star among thousands of others in the permanent night sky.

Past and Future Visits

No missions have reached Pluto yet.

Martian Jokes

1st Martian: I'm homesick.

2nd Martian: But this is your home.

1st Martian: I know, and I'm sick of it!

Why did the Martian have a blancmange in one ear
and a jelly in the other two?

She was a trifle deaf.

What did the policewoman say to the three-headed
Martian?

Hello, hello, hello!

How did the Martian stop a cold from going to
his chest?

He tied a knot in his neck.

What's a Martian's normal eyesight?

20-20-20 vision!

Chapter Seven
SPACE JUNK

SO, WHAT ELSE IS OUT THERE?

ARE YOU KIDDING? THERE'S TONS OF JUNK IN YOUR SOLAR SYSTEM!

Humans have launched lots of satellites into space and dumped lots of litter along the way. But that's not all. There are thousands of asteroids and comets and other weird objects hurtling around. In this chapter let's see just how choc full the Solar System really is!

Asteroids

These are lumps of rock and metal that orbit the Sun but they are too small to be proper planets, so they're called minor planets or asteroids. They are left over from when the Solar System was formed and some believe they are the remains of a planet that shattered billions of years ago.

The biggest one, Ceres, was also the first one to be discovered when G. Piazzi looked through his telescope on New Years Day 1801. It is about 1,000km (620 miles) wide.

If you put all the asteroids in a huge container, Ceres would take up a third of the total weight. Most of them range in size from pebbles upwards.

There are about 16 other asteroids that are over 240km (150 miles) wide and we know that they whizz around the Sun between Earth and Saturn.

Asteroids

Where are they?

Most of the asteroids live in the asteroid belt
between Mars and Jupiter but some of them have
hit the Earth in the past – we have the craters to
prove it. There's a great example in Arizona, USA,
called the Barringer Meteor Crater.

Top Three Asteroid Heavies

Ceres is the largest and first to be discovered.
Pallas is second largest and second to be
discovered – in 1802.
Vesta – is third largest.

Judgement Day

If a large asteroid (more than a quarter of a mile wide) hit the Earth it would be a global disaster. The impact would send dust into the air that would block out sunlight and we would be plunged into another ice age. Fortunately, the chances of it happening are very small — about once every 100,000 years.

GAMES LINK

Play Asteroids online
http://www.kidsastronomy.com/
asteroid/

Judgement Day

Don't get too smug, though. Smaller asteroids hit Earth once every 1,000 to 10,000 years, their impact enough to destroy a city or cause a terrible tidal wave. Scientists at NASA's Near Earth Asteroid Tracking (NEAT) programme are tracking the movements of about 160 of these Near Earth Objects (NEOs) right now and are searching for others. If we get about 40 years warning then there's a chance we may develop the technology to destroy it or send it off course.

COOL LINK
Visit the asteroid gallery at http://nssdc.gsfc. nasa.gov/photo_ gallery/photogallery- asteroids.html

Painting Asteroids

An asteroid first spotted in 1950 has a 1-in-300 chance of hitting the Earth in the year 2880. But NASA thinks that painting it might be enough to save the Earth!

Have they gone nuts? Why don't they just nuke it? It's not as crazy as it seems, because painting part of it would actually make it change its course as it absorbed less sunlight. Remember Solar Sails in chapter two?

Of course, it would only work over hundreds of years — so nuking them is always the best last resort.

Asteroid Maze

Can you fly your spaceship through the asteroid belt from Mars to Jupiter without hitting an asteroid?

Answer on page 184

Comets

Comets are dirty snowballs of frozen water, gas and dust, orbiting the Sun. We only notice them when they are near the Sun when they gain a tail up to 10 million km (6.2 million miles) long made of glowing dust particles.

Humans have known about comets for centuries. There are Chinese records of Halley's Comet going back to 240 BC.

It famously appeared in 1066 before the Battle of Hastings. It was so bright that it terrified millions of Europeans and is shown on the Bayeux Tapestry.

ITS NEXT APPEARANCE IS IN 2061. HOW OLD WILL YOU BE THEN?

HAROLD

Bad Omens

ONCE UPON A TIME, PEOPLE WERE VERY FRIGHTENED OF COMETS AND THOUGHT THEY BROUGHT BAD LUCK AND EVEN DISASTERS.

Even as recently as the Halley appearance in 1910, the detection of various gases in the comet tail gave rise to panic. Newspapers and magazines were full of dreadful stories, showing people poisoned in the streets by comet gases.

Even today some people expected the appearance of the Hale-Bopp comet in 1997 to mark the end of the world.

Counting Comets

About 900 large comets have been spotted. Of these about 180 are periodic (meaning they orbit in less than 200 years). But there are lots which pass by once every few thousand years.

COOL LINK
Make your own comet at http://amazing-space.stsci.edu/

EACH YEAR, ABOUT TEN MILLION SMALL COMETS HIT THE EARTH.

BUT THEY START TO BREAK APART ABOUT 1,300 km (800 MILES) AWAY.

BY THE TIME THEY REACH EARTH THEY HAVE TURNED INTO WATER VAPOUR - SO THEY ARE HARMLESS.

It's amazing to think that every few seconds a snowball the size of your house arrives in the atmosphere! Watch out if you're in a spacecraft, though! You are bound to run into a small comet on your travels through the Solar System.

Take a Shower

Meteor showers sometimes happen when the Earth passes through the tail of a comet.

The Perseid meteor shower happens every year between 9 and 13 August when the Earth passes through the orbit of the Swift-Tuttle Comet.

The Orionids meteor shower happens each October when Earth passes through the debris stream of Halley's Comet, and meteoroids hit the atmosphere at nearly 145,000km/h (90,000mph). Find the constellation of Orion and you'll be able to spot some.

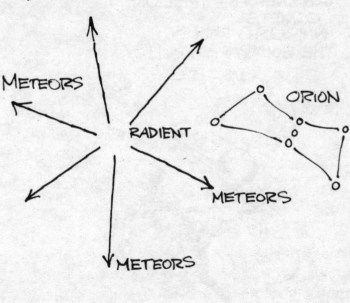

METEORS

RADIENT

ORION

METEORS

METEORS

EAST   ORIONID RADIENT   WEST

Belts & Clouds

Comets come from two places – the first is the Kuiper Belt out beyond Neptune. The second is an enormous cloud way beyond Pluto which surrounds the entire Solar System. Its existence was put forward by a Dutchman called Jan Oort in 1950 – the cloud is called the Oort cloud. Comets are nudged into the Solar System by the gravitational force of passing stars!

ASTRONOMERS ESTIMATE THERE ARE OVER ONE TRILLION COMETS WHIRLING ROUND THE SOLAR SYSTEM!

Big Bopper

Comet Hale-Bopp sparked an uproar when it was spotted by two amateur astronomers on 23 July 1995 because it was very bright and a long way away. That made it VERY big.

COOL LINK
See pics at http://www.jpl.nasa.gov/comet/images.html

The nucleus is about 40km (25 miles) wide, making it possibly the largest comet known. Halley's Comet measures about 8 by 16 km (5 by 10 miles).

Hale-Bopp was visible from Earth with the naked eye during March 1997 but now that it has whizzed past at 200,000km/h (125,000mph) we won't see it again for another 3,000 years! The last time Hale-Bopp visited us the Egyptian pyramids were being built 4,200 years ago.

Time Capsules

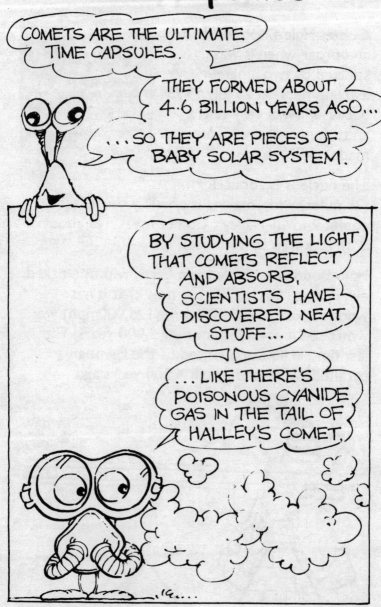

COMETS ARE THE ULTIMATE TIME CAPSULES.

THEY FORMED ABOUT 4·6 BILLION YEARS AGO...

...SO THEY ARE PIECES OF BABY SOLAR SYSTEM.

BY STUDYING THE LIGHT THAT COMETS REFLECT AND ABSORB, SCIENTISTS HAVE DISCOVERED NEAT STUFF...

...LIKE THERE'S POISONOUS CYANIDE GAS IN THE TAIL OF HALLEY'S COMET.

Comet Puzzle

Look closely at the tails of these ten comets.
Which is the odd one out?

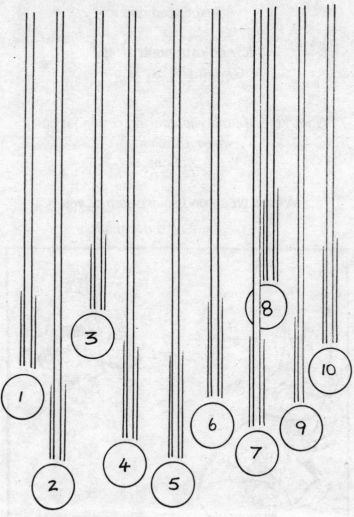

Answer on page 184

Space Jokes

What sort of sentence would you get if you broke
the law of gravity?

A suspended one.

How do astronauts sleep?

With their eyes shut.

What kind of umbrella does an astronaut carry
when it's raining?

A wet one.

What's green and squirts jam at you?

An alien eating a doughnut.

Catch a Comet

Wouldn't it be amazing if we could catch a comet? Ha! It's been done already using a spy plane called the U2 which can fly really high to catch comet dust on its sticky hull!

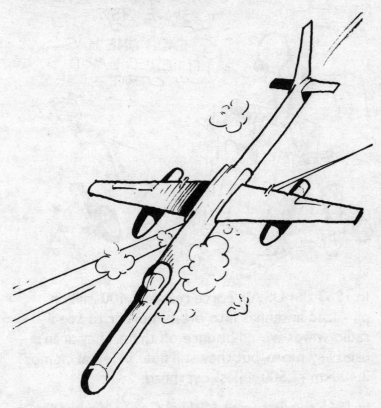

But best of all, the Rosetta Mission will be launched in 2003, aiming to meet Comet Wirtannen in 2011 and actually send two craft on to the comet's surface!

Human Junk

In 1963 the US Air Force released 400 million pin-sized antennas into orbit in order to see if radio waves would bounce off them. They aren't used any more, but they still float in lethal clumps 2,400km (1,500 miles) overhead.

In 1965 the astronaut Michael Collins 'dropped' a camera while on a space walk. Many spacecraft lose bits – heat shield tiles, nuts, bolts, gloves. Some Soviet spy satellites are leaking coolant into space that now floats around like lethal frozen golf balls.

Human Junk

Much of this stuff has fallen back to Earth and burned up in the atmosphere but there is still about 1.8 million kg (4 million lb) of this weird crud travelling at up to 28,000km/h (17,500mph).

It's now a real threat to spaceships like the shuttle and the International Space Station. Even the smallest fragment can be dangerous – a tiny speck of paint from a satellite once chipped out a quarter-inch of Space Shuttle window.

As with most pollution, the dangers were ignored for years, but now the problem is so big that the US Space Surveillance Network has to track more than 9,000 objects bigger than a baseball, in case they hit the shuttle, but there are estimated to be over 100,000 smaller objects they can't even detect.

IT'S TIME TO SHAPE UP BEFORE IT'S TOO BIG A PROBLEM TO CLEAN UP!

Scary Junk

THE 130-TON MIR SPACE STATION CHUCKED 200 RUBBISH BAGS INTO SPACE DURING ITS FIRST TEN YEARS OF OPERATION.

IT DUMPED ITSELF INTO THE SOUTH PACIFIC ON 23 MARCH 2001.

A SECRET SOVIET SATELLITE, COSMOS 954, WAS FUELLED BY A NUCLEAR REACTOR. IN JANUARY 1978, IT CRASHED IN A REMOTE PART OF ARCTIC CANADA. THE CIA QUICKLY SWEPT UP THIS LETHAL RADIOACTIVE WRECKAGE AND BILLED THE USSR $6,041,174.70.

Scary Junk

TO LEARN ABOUT SPACE JUNK, NASA LAUNCHED YET ANOTHER SATELLITE – THE LONG DURATION EXPOSURE FACILITY (LDEF) IN 1984. AFTER SPENDING SIX YEARS AS A MULTI-MILLION POUND COSMIC DART BOARD, IT RETURNED TO EARTH IN 1990 WHERE SCIENTISTS COUNTED OVER 19,000 TINY IMPACT CRATERS!

IN 1965, EDWARD WHITE, LOST A GLOVE DURING A SPACE WALK. IT STAYED IN ORBIT FOR A MONTH, TRAVELLING AT 28,000/KM/H – THE FASTEST AND MOST DANGEROUS ITEM OF CLOTHING EVER.

THERE ARE OVER 2,700 SATELLITES ORBITING THE EARTH.

Galactic Giggles

What do you call a chicken from outer space?
An eggs-traterrestrial.

How does the Solar System hold up its trousers?
With an asteroid belt.

What do you call an alien star ship that drips water?
A crying saucer!

What did the space scientist find in his frying pan?
An unidentified frying object.

Faster Than Light?

OK, then why not travel FASTER than the speed of light? Well, scientists may be proved wrong in the future, but at the moment Einstein's Theory of Relativity tells us that nothing can travel faster than light – it would be breaking the laws that rule the whole universe!

Or would it? In the early 1990s Miguel Alcubierre's theory made scientists think again. He suggested a Warp Drive that would scrunch up space in front of a spacecraft and stretch it behind, while the spacecraft sits in its own bubble of space-time. This is a lot like the warp drive of *Star Trek*, but it requires anti-matter, which we don't have in this universe! And besides, his calculations were wrong. Shucks!

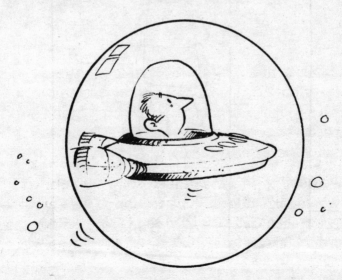

Chill Out

There's always ... Cryogenics. That means freezing the body or hibernation. Maybe it's possible, maybe not.

Your main problem is that you are made up mostly of water, which makes cells rupture when they freeze. Then there's the little matter of waking up after a refreshing 200-year nap to the thought that everyone you ever knew on Earth is long dead!

Time Travel

Ever since H. G. Wells wrote his book *The Time Machine* humans have been fascinated by time travel. But is it possible?

Einstein's Theory of Relativity says that time slows down for anything travelling near the speed of light, so time travellers would not age as much as the people they leave behind on Earth.

If they travelled right at the speed of light they would not age at all because time would stop. If they travelled faster than that they would start to go back in time.

Time Travel

Trouble is, it takes an infinite amount of energy to reach the speed of light! And also, at the speed of light your own mass would be infinite! And you just can't travel faster than the speed of light.

Plus, even if you were travelling close to light speed anything you collided with – even something as small as an atom – would make your ship disintegrate.

Finally, how do you get back to the future? The above method may take you back in time, but as far as science can tell, there is no way of returning.

Bending Space

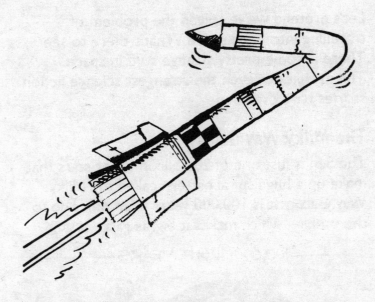

This means actually distorting time and space to form a short cut between two places. Einstein came up with an amazing idea that very heavy objects actually bend space – the bigger the mass the more space is bent. In theory a wormhole could appear where two or more massive bodies warp space.

Think of space as a balloon. If you push your fists into either side it is possible to get both sides of the balloon to touch – making the distance between these two points zero. Much quicker than travelling round one half of the balloon to get to the other side! Now there's an exciting idea!

What's Out There?

Let's pretend we've solved the problem of travelling into deep space. What's there to see? There is some pretty strange stuff in space. Things that not even the strangest science fiction stories have dreamed.

The Milky Way Galaxy

The Sun is just one of 200 billion other stars that make up a huge spiral pattern called the Milky Way Galaxy. It is 100,000 years from one side to the other – which makes it big, as galaxies go.

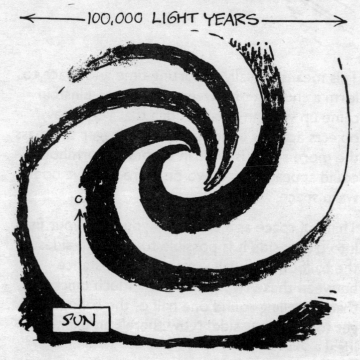

← —— 100,000 LIGHT YEARS —— →

SUN

Milky Way

It has three main parts: a *disk*, a central *bulge*, and a *halo*. The disk of the Milky Way has four spiral arms made up mostly of 'young' stars between a million and ten billion years old.

The Solar System lies near the edge of one of these arms, called the Orion arm because it contains the bright stars found in the constellation Orion. Stars are spread far apart in this region of the galaxy.

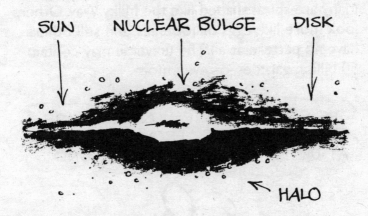

The bulge is a dense central clump of old stars about 10 billion years old. A monstrous black hole may lurk at the centre of the bulge. The black hole may be a million times heavier than the Sun.

The halo is a fuzzy cloud of the oldest known stars (10–15 billion years) which surrounds the disk.

Beyond The Milky Way

Space doesn't stop there! The universe is filled with galaxies — 'cities of stars' like the Milky Way. Each galaxy contains millions or billions of stars.

The first galaxy other than our own was 'discovered' by Edwin Hubble in October 1923, when he realised that the Andromeda Nebula was actually a galaxy outside the Milky Way. Since then astronomers have found that galaxies come in many shapes, sizes and colours.

Many are spiral shaped like the Milky Way. Others look more like eggs or footballs, and still others have no pattern at all. The universe may contain 50 billion galaxies, or even more.

THE GALAXIES IN THE UNIVERSE ARE TRAVELLING AWAY FROM EACH OTHER AT UP TO 112,651 Km PER SECOND.

Galaxy Spotting

Spiral

Flat disks of stars with bright bulges in their centres and spiral arms.

Elliptical

Look like fat, fuzzy eggs or footballs.
The largest galaxies in the universe are giant ellipticals. They can contain a trillion stars or more, and span as much as two million light-years – about 20 times the width of the Milky Way.

Irregular

These galaxies have no identifiable shape and the stars are spread randomly.

Pulsars

PULSating stARS are among the weirdest objects in the galaxy (apart from aliens!). They are formed when a massive star, much bigger than our Sun, runs out of fuel and explodes.

All that is left after this explosion (called a supernova) is a super-dense neutron star.

IF YOU COULD SCOOP UP A TEASPOON OF A NEUTRON STAR IT WOULD WEIGH ABOUT A BILLION TONS.

A neutron star has very strong gravity which makes it shine more like a torch than a light bulb. Now imagine this torch spinning around very fast and you have a pulsar – a kind of cosmic lighthouse, flashing on and off many times a second.

Black Holes

YOU'VE HEARD OF THESE? YOU PROBABLY KNOW THEM AS GIANT COSMIC VACUUM CLEANERS— SWALLOWING ANYTHING THAT GOES NEAR. WELL, YOU'RE RIGHT.

There are two main types of black hole: stellar and super-massive. A stellar black hole is the remains of a large collapsed star (about ten times the mass of the Sun).

But scientists think there are super-massive black holes at the centre of every galaxy, about a million times the mass of the Sun.

Black Holes

Black holes are regions of space which have so much mass that not even light can escape their gravitational pull.

In chapter two we saw that to escape the Earth's gravity a rocket needs to travel faster than the Earth's 'escape velocity'. In a black hole that escape velocity is faster than the speed of light.

Nothing can escape. But you will be able to see all the stuff being sucked in – oddly making a black hole one of the brightest things in the galaxy!

Stay away from the light! If you did fall in at first you'd be pleasantly weightless, but as you got closer you'd be stretched like chewing gum until you were ripped apart into billions of atoms. You have been warned!

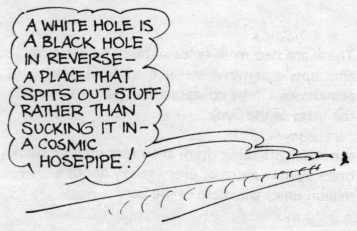

A WHITE HOLE IS A BLACK HOLE IN REVERSE – A PLACE THAT SPITS OUT STUFF RATHER THAN SUCKING IT IN – A COSMIC HOSEPIPE!

Aliens

IF YOU ARE LUCKY (OR UNLUCKY) ENOUGH TO MEET ALIENS, THERE'S LOTS YOU SHOULD KNOW BEFORE JUMPING FORWARD WITH A BIG SMILE AND A BAG OF COOKIES!

COOKIES

SETI

At the moment scientists search for intelligent life by using radio telescopes tuned to detect the emissions of other technologically advanced civilisations. (Projects involving the **S**earch for **ExtraT**errestrial **I**ntelligence are referred to by the acronym SETI.)

During 2001 scientists discovered over 50 planets orbiting stars other than the Sun. But there are millions more. Some may even support life!

Hot Stuff

Even on Earth, creatures have been discovered surviving in places that humans used to think were impossible to live in.

Crabs and giant worms have been discovered several miles underwater on the sea bed. There is no sunlight, but these animals get their energy and food from vents where extremely hot water (up to 350°C) bursts out from inside the Earth.

Scientists used to think that nothing could survive without getting energy from the Sun, but these creatures somehow manage to.

This means that it is also possible that there is life on planets far away from stars, or on planets with very tough environments like ice or extreme heat.

Alien Appearance

On Earth animals look different because they have adapted to different environments. If you want to imagine what an alien might look like, then first you've got to imagine where they live.

Here are three planets. See if you can match each alien to its correct planet.

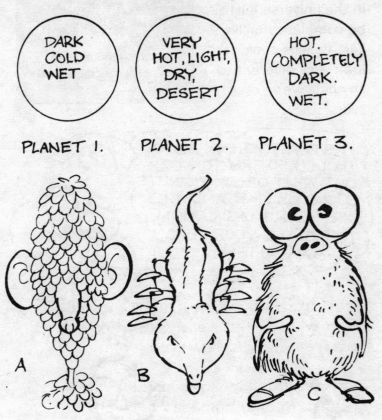

DARK COLD WET

VERY HOT, LIGHT, DRY, DESERT

HOT. COMPLETELY DARK. WET.

PLANET 1.   PLANET 2.   PLANET 3.

A

B

C

Answer on page 184

Alien Appearance

You see how it works? You don't need eyes when it's completely dark. But you might need big ears instead. Who needs fur in the desert? Where would you need huge eyes – dark or light?

You can see that because other planets in the universe might be completely unlike Earth, aliens could look very different to anything we've ever seen.

COOL LINK

Create your own alien at http://www.space.com/php/entertainment/

IT'S FUN TO THINK ABOUT THOUGH, SO TRY TO WORK OUT WHAT OTHER PLANETS COULD BE LIKE, AND THEN USE YOUR IMAGINATION TO CREATE YOUR VERY OWN ALIEN.

Feed Me!

This mean looking extra-terrestrial will eat you in five minutes unless you can figure out what to give him instead.

Answer on page 184

Close Encounters

Humans who claim to have met alien visitors to Earth often describe one of three types:

Grays

Short, bald grey beings with almond-shaped eyes and large bulbous heads.

Nordics

These look very human – they can blend in easily, so we wouldn't even guess they were from another galaxy.

Close Encounters

Monsters and Reptilians

Creatures depicted in films like *The Thing* or *Men In Black*. These are less common! Maybe because humans don't live to tell their tale!

MAYBE THEY HAVE ALREADY, MAYBE THEY DON'T WANT TO ... MAYBE WE WOULDN'T RECOGNISE THEM EVEN IF THEY DID. WHAT DOES A BEETLE KNOW ABOUT YOU, OTHER THAN SOMETHING IS CASTING A SHADOW!

Fermi Paradox

If extraterrestrial life exists in the universe, why haven't they contacted us yet?

Space Jokes

Sherlock Holmes and Doctor Watson are on a camping expedition, but in the middle of the night Holmes wakes Watson up and asks him a question.

Holmes: Watson, look up at the stars and tell me what you deduce.

Watson: I see millions of stars, and if there are millions of stars, and if even a few of those have planets, it is quite likely there are some planets like Earth, and if there are a few planets like Earth out there there might also be life.

Holmes: Watson, you idiot! Somebody stole our tent.

Chapter Nine
TO INFINITY AND BEYOND

IF YOU THINK THE LAST CHAPTER WAS WEIRD, YOU AIN'T SEEN NOTHING YET!

This final chapter looks at the origin of the entire universe. Where it began and where it will end. Get ready for a journey through the minds of some of the most brilliant scientists the Earth has ever known.

Big Bang Theory

This is the most popular theory about how the universe was born. It says that about 15 billion years ago the whole universe was packed into a single atom! This atom is called a 'singularity'. At the singularity time did not exist – it hadn't started yet.

Then, there was a HUGE explosion – called the Big Bang. In less than one thousandth of a second the universe doubled in size over a hundred times to about 2/3 of a mile across.

BIG B

The temperature of the universe was trillions of degrees!

Big Bang Theory

Ever since then all the matter in the universe has continued to fly outwards very fast and is cooling down.

Scientists have worked out that one second after the Big Bang the temperature had already dropped to 10 billion degrees. After three minutes the temperature was a mere 1 billion degrees!

The universe was still so dense that the first light didn't appear until 300,000 years later.

However in billions of years all this matter will slow down, stop and start being pulled back to the singularity – the whole process will go backwards as the universe is sucked back into one atom. This is called the Big Crunch.

Big Bang Theory

The trouble with the Big Bang theory is that some scientists believe that certain processes in the universe just haven't been given enough time to happen.

For example, judging by the speed at which the Milky Way galaxy is rotating, it can only have had a chance to rotate about fifty times during the last 15 billion years, which some scientists don't think is nearly enough time for it to have formed into its spiral shape.

Scientist Quotations

SOMETIMES I THINK WE'RE ALONE IN THE UNIVERSE, AND SOMETIMES I THINK WE'RE NOT. IN EITHER CASE THE IDEA IS QUITE STAGGERING.

ARTHUR C. CLARK —

PUT THREE GRAINS OF SAND INSIDE A VAST CATHEDRAL, AND THE CATHEDRAL WILL BE MORE CLOSELY PACKED WITH SAND THAN SPACE IS WITH STARS.

SIR JAMES JEANS —

JIM — A BRAINY THING!

SPACE ISN'T REMOTE AT ALL. IT'S ONLY AN HOUR'S DRIVE AWAY IF YOUR CAR COULD GO STRAIGHT UPWARDS.

SIR FRED HOYLE —

175

Theory Of Everything

Wouldn't it be nice to have one theory that explained everything in the universe. Dream on, you might say, but scientists have been searching for just that for centuries.

Albert Einstein was actually working hard on his own theory of everything when he died.

But in the last few years something very exciting has happened that, for the moment anyway, offers the closest thing to this dream.

AND IT ALL STARTED WITH A PIECE OF STRING.

YEP!

String Theory

This is an amazing new way of looking at how everything in the universe is built. We all know that matter is made up of tiny particles called atoms, but string theory says these are actually stretched into strings.

When these strings vibrate they produce matter – in the same way that when the strings of a violin are played they vibrate to produce lots of different notes and sound which we call music.

So matter is like music played on an incredible collection of cosmic strings! Hmmm. Far out!

The trouble was, when the same scientists tried to make String Theory fit neatly with the Big Bang they ended up with five different string theories – it was no longer the single theory of everything. Until ...

The Eleventh Dimension

. . . scientists invented the eleventh dimension!

We are used to talking about three dimensions:

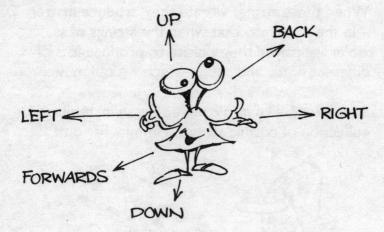

Albert Einstein added a fourth dimension, time, and over the years another six dimensions were either discovered or invented. All were explained by very complicated maths that only a handful of people in the world can understand!

Pretty soon there were ten dimensions and still String Theory just didn't fit in with the Big Bang. So scientists invented another dimension, the eleventh dimension, and suddenly everything magically worked.

The Eleventh Dimension

In the eleventh dimension strings join up –
knitted together to make an infinite number of
silky sheets, infinite in size but only a trillionth of
a millimetre thick.

Our universe is just one of many moving through
the eleventh dimension like a wave through a silk
sheet.

Parallel Universes

And if that isn't crazy enough, what do you think happens when two of these sheets touch? Why, there's a Big Bang and a new universe is formed. So the Big Bang didn't just happen once – it happens all the time!

The idea of parallel universes used to be the stuff of science fiction, but now mathematics can be used to show that there may be an infinite number of parallel universes – some of which have you in a different form, some don't have you at all.

So where are these other universes? Less than a fraction of a millimetre away.

The Truth Is Out There

With every new scientific discovery humans have had to rethink their place in the heavens. At first they thought theirs was the only planet, then they discovered more planets, then more solar systems, more galaxies and now even more universes! Where will it end?

One thing is for certain: whatever is out there is an enormous, strange and wonderful place (or places) that will probably always be just beyond complete understanding.

EVEN MINE!

Homeward Bound

WELL, I HOPE YOU'VE ENJOYED YOUR TOUR AROUND YOUR GALAXY AND BEYOND.
I'M OFF HOME.
WHO KNOWS, IF YOU BECOME AN ASTRONAUT, SOMEDAY WE MAY MEET AGAIN!
BYE!

Answers

Page 31 Rocket Puzzle

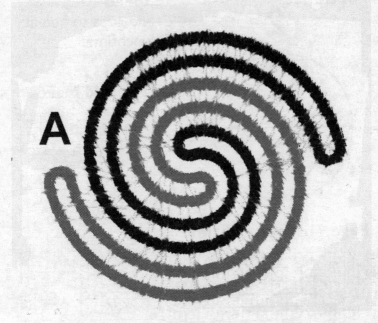

A

Page 38 Weight Puzzle
The astronaut weighs 128kg (284lb).

Page 57 Solar Panels Puzzle
Shuttle A is carrying the correct payload. A quick solution is to count the total number of panels, which should add up to 45.

Page 63 Space Puzzle
They must stand back to back.

Answers

Page 65 Space Walk Puzzle

2

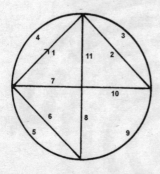

Page 91 Moon Puzzle

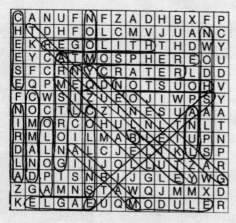

Page 101 Big Star, Little Star

They are the same size.

Page 105 Light Speed

She goes to bed at lunchtime!

Page 133 Asteroid Maze

Page 141 Comet Puzzle

Number 9

Page 165 Alien Appearance

1C, 2B, 3A

Page 167 Feed Me!

Doughnuts